Nice

A concise and Detailed Itinerary Handbook to a
Memorable Adventure, Discovery and Insider's
Experiences

BONUS:

- Itinerary
- Useful Phrases
- Family Vacation
- Solo Traveler
- Romantic Adventure
- Traveling with Pets
- Delectable Images

NICE
Travel Guide
2023

Elis Tello Rios

A concise and Detailed Itinerary handbook to a Memorable Adventure, Discovery and Insider's Experiences

Elis Tello Rios

Table of Contents

INTRODUCTION

Welcome to Nice

I found myself surrounded by the vivid hues and alluring fragrances of the French Riviera as the warm Mediterranean sun touched my skin. As I left for my much-anticipated vacation in Nice, there was a palpable feeling of excitement and expectation in the air. The city drew me in with its assurances of stunning scenery, extensive history, and a wide range of life-changing encounters.

I couldn't help but experience a wave of elation as I strolled down the Promenade des Anglais, the famous palm-lined avenue that extended along the blue ocean. I was surrounded by the bustling environment as both residents and visitors enjoyed the relaxed beauty of the city. The atmosphere of Nice was contagious, as shown by the animated conversation in the sidewalk cafés and the laughter that resounded through the Old Town's cobblestone streets.

I stumbled into a treasure trove of undiscovered jewels while exploring the Vieux Nice's twisting lanes. The colorful marketplaces provide a variety of mouthwatering fragrances and fresh goods. A sensory feast was further enhanced by the wafting aroma of freshly baked baguettes and the sight of craftsmen fervently creating their goods.

I became involved in the community by enjoying the delectable treats of traditional Niçois cuisine and indulging in the renowned rosé wines of the area. Nice captured my heart and stoked my spirit of adventure, from lazy days spent lazing on the pebbly beaches to adventurous excursions along the cliffs.

As I offer my experiences, insider knowledge, and thorough itineraries to help you make the most of your wonderful holiday in this gem of the French Riviera, I invite you to join me on this intriguing voyage via the pages of the Nice Travel Guide 2023.

1.2 About this Guide

Thanks for Choosing this Nice Travel Guide 2023! This thorough guide is intended to provide you with a clear and thorough itinerary guidebook for a great journey of discovery and insider experiences in Nice, a stunning city on the French Riviera.

This book strives to be your go-to resource, delivering insightful advice and useful tips to make your vacation to Nice unique, whether you're a first-time visitor or a seasoned traveler. We offer everything you need, from seeing the fascinating Old Town and soaking up the sun on the breathtaking beaches to indulging in delectable food and soaking up the lively local culture.

1.3 How to Use This Guide

a) Table of Contents: To receive an idea of the subjects covered, see the table of contents. You may use it to rapidly locate certain portions of interest.

b) Each chapter focuses on a different part of your vacation, such as touring Nice, eating and nightlife, outdoor activities, cultural experiences, shopping, practical information, itinerary recommendations, and further resources. Some subsections go further into certain themes inside each chapter.

c) Find highlights and insider advice throughout the book by keeping an eye out for them. These will provide you with insightful advice and local knowledge to improve your vacation experience

d) Delectable Images: To assist you in visualizing the city, its attractions, and the suggested itineraries, we have included a few images. They'll make it easier for you to navigate Nice and organize your schedule.

Remember that this travel guide is just a tool to help you plan your trip and to inspire you; the final decision over what to do and see is yours. As you go out on a mission of discovery across the alluring city of Nice, let the adventure begin!

Chapter 2: Getting Started

2.1 The Best Time to Visit

It's crucial to organize your vacation to Nice taking your tastes and the activities you want to participate in into account. Nice has moderate winters and hot summers thanks to its Mediterranean environment. Here are the various seasons' top points:

Spring (March to May): Nice experiences lovely weather, blossoming flowers, and fewer tourists throughout the spring season. It's a great time to visit the city's attractions, engage in outdoor activities, and go to community events.

Summer (June to August): With pleasant temperatures and plenty of sunlight, summer is Nice's busiest travel season. The city comes to life with events and a thriving nightlife, and the beaches are crowded. However, expect more people and more expensive items.

Fall (September to November): Compared to the summer, Nice's autumn provides excellent weather and fewer visitors. It's a terrific time to go sightseeing, discover other cultures, and engage in outdoor pursuits like hiking. Early in the season, the water is still warm enough for swimming.

Winter (December to February): Although Nice has moderate winters with few lows below zero, this is the slowest travel period. The benefit is that fewer people are visiting the city's cultural attractions, such as its museums and art galleries. In the neighboring mountains, it's a great season for winter activities as well.

2.2 Visa Requirements

Check the visa requirements for your country of residence before visiting Nice. It is not necessary to get a visa to enter the country for a brief visit if you are an EU or Schengen Area national. Visitors from outside the EU should consult their own country's French consulate or embassy to find out whether they need a visa to enter Nice.

2.3 Currency and Financial Issues

The Euro (EUR) is the official currency of Nice and all of France. For minor transactions and in case you come across businesses that do not take credit cards, it is good to have some Euros on hand. The city has a large number of ATMs, and most businesses take credit cards.

Additionally, it's a good idea to let your bank know about your vacation plans so they can make sure your cards will function overseas and find out if there are any potential international transaction fees or currency conversion penalties.

2.4 Transportation Options

Nice boasts an efficient public transportation system that makes it simple to travel inside the city and outside of it. Consider the following possibilities for transportation:

a) Public Transportation: Lignes d'Azur, which runs buses and trams in Nice, offers an effective system for getting about town. Access to different areas of the city and nearby towns is made simple by these alternatives.

b) Taxis and ridesharing services are both widely used and practical for moving about Nice. Taxis are readily accessible across the city.

c) Electric scooter rentals and bike sharing are available in Nice, giving visitors an enjoyable and environmentally responsible alternative to see the city at their leisure.

d) Nice is a walking city, especially in the central districts. You can take in the splendor of the city while you explore since many of the major sights are within easy walking distance of one another.

Several vehicle rental companies are available in Nice whether you want the convenience of a car or want to go outside of the city.

2.5 Accommodations Options

Nice has a variety of lodging choices to accommodate all tastes and price ranges. Here are a few well-liked options:

a) Hotels: Nice boasts a wide range of hotels spread out over the city, including boutique hotels, luxury resorts, and affordable choices.

b) Apartments and Vacation homes: Renting an apartment or a home away from home might provide you with a more autonomous and intimate experience. Apartments, villas, and studios are just a few of the alternatives that are available on several sites.

c) Hostels: For tourists on a tight budget, Nice features several hostels that provide reasonable lodging and an opportunity to socialize with other travelers.

d) Nice boasts exquisite bed & breakfast places that provide a more individualized and private experience.

e) Guesthouses & Pension Houses: These more intimate, family-run accommodations provide a homey feel and are often found in the center of the city or quaint areas.

f) Consider features like location, facilities, and closeness to attractions when selecting a place to stay, as well as reviews and ratings from prior visitors.

You are prepared to begin your experience in Nice with this crucial information in mind. Enjoy the journey!

A concise and Detailed Itinerary Handbook to a
Memorable Adventure, Discovery and Insider's
Experiences

BONUS:

• Itinerary
• Useful Phrases
• Family Vacation
• Solo Traveler
• Romantic Adventure
• Traveling with Pets
• Delectable Images

NICE
Travel Guide
2023

Elis Tello Rios

Chapter 3: Getting to Know Nice

3.1 Overview of Nice

Nice, a city in France, is a master at fusing its past, present, and future with its surrounding natural beauty. It has long been a popular travel destination due to its Mediterranean temperature, palm-lined boulevards, and turquoise seas. Nice is the ideal vacation destination because it combines old-world elegance with contemporary energy.

The city is renowned for its beautiful coastline, bustling markets, and extensive architectural history. It is possible for visitors to Nice to fully immerse themselves in the region's history and creative riches because of the city's abundance of museums, art galleries, and cultural attractions.

The finest of Niçois cuisine, which mixes Provençal and Italian influences, is also included in the city's eating scene, teasing the taste buds of food lovers.

3.2 Top Attractions in Nice

3.2.1 Promenade des Anglais

The Baie des Anges (Bay of Angels) beachfront promenade is known as the Promenade des

Anglais. This charming avenue is a well-liked location for strolls, cycling, and people-watching and provides breathtaking views of the Mediterranean Sea. Palm trees, opulent hotels, cafés, and beaches surround the promenade, enticing guests to unwind and take in the lively ambiance.

3.2.2 Vieux Nice (Old Town)

Experience Old Town, often known as Vieux Nice, for what it is. Its curving, meandering lanes are lined with vibrant squares, beautiful architecture, and quaint shops. Discover the vibrant Cours Saleya market, where you can purchase local delicacies, flowers, and fresh fruit. Explore the elaborate Cathédrale Sainte-Réparate and the Nice History Museum to learn more about the history and culture of the region.

3.3 Castle Hill (Colline du Château)

Castle Hill, which rises above the city, provides sweeping views of Nice and the nearby beach. Although the ancient castle is no longer there, the hill is still a well-liked tourist destination. Either use the elevator or the steps to go to the top. Take a picnic, explore the lovely gardens, and take stunning cityscape pictures. Don't overlook the famous waterfall, which is a cool place to be in the summer.

3.2.4 Musée Matisse

Art lovers must visit the Musée Matisse, which is devoted to the creations of the famous artist Henri Matisse. The museum, which is housed in a lovely 17th-century villa, has a sizable collection of Matisse's artwork, sculptures, sketches, and personal effects. It provides an engrossing tour of the artist's life and his developing creative style.

3.2.5 Place Masséna

Place Masséna, a bustling plaza in the center of Nice, is well-known for its gorgeous architecture, fountains, and lively ambiance. Admire the famed Apollo's Fountain and the beautiful red buildings with neoclassical façade. The square is a bustling gathering place for both residents and tourists throughout the year because of the many events and festivals it sponsors.

These are just a handful of Nice's major tourist destinations. The Russian Orthodox Cathedral, the Musée d'Art Moderne et d'Art Contemporain (MAMAC), and the Musée des Beaux-Arts de Nice (Fine Arts Museum) are just a few of the many attractions the city has to offer. Give yourself plenty of time to explore the city's hidden attractions and get engrossed in its distinctive atmosphere.

3.3 Hidden Gems and Local Attractions

Be careful to go off the main route while touring Nice to find some of the local favorites and undiscovered attractions. These treasures provide you with a look into real Niçois culture and give you special travel experiences.

3.3.1 Cours Saleya Market

Beyond its fame, the Old Town's Cours Saleya Market is a veritable treasure trove of regional treats. Investigate the market first thing in the morning to take in its vibrant atmosphere and discover fresh vegetables, aromatic flowers, and local specialties. Try the socca, a popular street snack made from chickpea flour, or treat yourself to some renowned lavender honey.

3.3.2 Liberation Market

Visit the Liberation Market in the Liberation district for a more authentic experience. Fresh fruits, vegetables, cheeses, and other delectable foods are available at this busy market in a dazzling variety. It's a great spot to meet locals, try regional cuisine, and experience the true Niçois atmosphere.

3.3.3 Parc de la Colline du Château

Even though Castle Hill is a well-liked tourist destination, the Parc de la Colline du Château conceals a serene haven away from the masses. Escape to this tranquil park to take in the rich vegetation, secret pathways, and stunning city views. It's the ideal location for a picnic, a calm walk, or just to relax and take in the beauty of nature.

3.3.4 Le Port Lympia

Le Port Lympia, the port in Nice, offers a true marine experience. Take a stroll around the port, see the fisherman at work, and take in the sight of the opulent yachts and vibrant fishing vessels. Embrace the colorful atmosphere of the port as you indulge in fresh seafood at one of the waterfront restaurants or grab a drink at a neighborhood bar.

3.4 Day Trips from Nice

Nice has many attractions, but while you're there, explore the lovely environs and go on day excursions to other places. Here are a few well-liked day excursion ideas:

3.4.1 Monaco

The opulent city-state of Monaco is just a short drive from Nice. Visit the Prince's Palace, see the lavish Casino de Monte-Carlo, and stroll through Monaco-Ville's quaint cobblestone alleyways. Don't pass up the opportunity to see the daily ceremonial of the Changing of the Guard that takes place outside the palace.

3.4.2 Cannes

Cannes, a coastal town famous for its film festival, is renowned for its glitz and stunning beaches. Take a stroll down La Croisette, the city's principal promenade, which is surrounded by opulent hotels and designer shops. Visit the Film Festival Palace to experience the chic atmosphere of this well-known Mediterranean location.

3.4.3 Antibes

Take in the allure of Antibes, a little town with a fascinating history. Visit the Picasso Museum, which is located in the Château Grimaldi, and explore the beautifully restored walls that encircle the Old Town. Take a walk around the bustling market areas, check out the marina, and unwind on a sandy beach.

3.4.4 Eze Village

Discover the allure of Eze Village, which is set on a mountaintop with a view of the Mediterranean. Explore the winding medieval lanes, savor the stone buildings, and take in the expansive views from the Jardin Exotique. Discover the lovely artisan stores and galleries and get lost in this gorgeous village's medieval ambiance.

These day excursions from Nice allow you to discover the French Riviera's varied natural beauties and give your schedule a little diversity. Make enduring memories of your trip in the area by selecting the locations that most interest you.

Chapter 4: Dining and Nightlife

4.1 Typical Nice Food

Nice is famed for its delectable food, which mixes Provence and Italian tastes with Mediterranean ones. The following traditional foods are a must-try:

a) Socca: A chickpea-based pancake that is often eaten as a street food snack.

b) Salade Niçoise: A light salad containing tuna, hard-boiled eggs, olives, and anchovies that are tossed in olive oil.

c) A tasty vegetable stew cooked with tomatoes, bell peppers, zucchini, eggplant, and herbs is called ratatouille.

d) A typical Niçois onion tart with a thin crust and toppings of caramelized onions, anchovies, and olives is known as pissaladière.

e) A robust sandwich called a pan bagnat, which is sometimes served with a drizzle of olive oil, is made with tuna, veggies, olives, and hard-boiled eggs.

4.2 Top Cafes and Restaurants

There are many excellent cafés and restaurants in Nice that provide fantastic eating experiences. Here are some suggestions:

4.2.1 Le Bistro du Fromager

Le Bistro du Fromager is a must-visit if you like cheese. In addition to a large assortment of cheeses from France and other countries, this charming café specializes in handcrafted cheeses. With a bottle of wine and a cheese plate, you may experience the tastes and textures of the best cheeses.

4.2.2 La Merenda

La Merenda is a well-known restaurant serving genuine Niçois food. Traditional cuisine prepared with fresh, regional ingredients is served at this modest, little eatery in Old Town. Even though the menu is always changing, you can count on tasty meals like stuffed veggies, braised meats, and warming stews.

4.2.3 Lou Pilha Leva

Visit Lou Pilha Leva for a relaxed dining experience that focuses on local food. Socca, pissaladière, and another traditional fare from the region of Nice are available at this quaint restaurant. The staff is renowned for their great friendliness, and the setting is cozy and welcoming.

4.3 Pubs and Clubs

Nice comes alive after sunset with a thriving nightlife scene. Here are some places to check out for pubs and clubs:

4.3.1 Wayne's Bar

Popular for its laid-back atmosphere and live music, Wayne's Bar has both. Drink a variety of drinks, artisan beers, and wines while taking part in open mic evenings or listening to local musicians. It's a terrific location to relax and interact because of the welcoming environment and helpful personnel.

4.3.2 Le Ghost

The popular nightclub Le Ghost is situated in the center of Nice. With a blend of dance, hip-hop, and electronic music, it provides a vibrant environment. Enjoy the vibrant atmosphere of this well-liked establishment as you dance the night away on the roomy dance floor.

4.3.3 High Club

One of Nice's most recognized nightclubs, High Club, is the place to go for a fancy night out. High Club draws revelers from near and far because of its several dance floors, VIP spaces, and outstanding DJs. A memorable nightlife experience is guaranteed by the club's themed evenings and unique events.

Nice provides a range of eating and nightlife alternatives to suit various interests and preferences, whether you're searching for a quiet restaurant, an energetic bar, or a throbbing nightclub. Enjoy the regional food, drink local wines, and take part in the exciting nightlife of this alluring city.

Chapter 5: Outdoor Adventures

5.1 Beaches in Nice

Nice is renowned for having stunning beaches around the Mediterranean Sea. Popular beaches to visit are listed below:

a) Plage Publique Beau Rivage: This public beach provides a combination of pebbles and sand and is close to the Old Town. It offers breathtaking views of the Promenade des Anglais and is conveniently located.

b) Castel Plage: This exclusive beach provides a serene atmosphere and first-rate facilities. It is located below Castle Hill. On the beach, dine as you relax on lounge chairs and take in the beautiful scenery.

c) Blue Beach: Known for its pristine seas, Blue Beach has both public and private spaces. It is a well-liked location for water sports, swimming, and tanning.

d) Coco Beach: Coco Beach provides a more tranquil ambiance and is encircled by cliffs and rich vegetation. It is tucked away from the city core. It's the perfect place to unwind and be alone.

5.2 Water Sports and Recreation

Nice has a lot to offer in terms of water sports and activities. Popular choices comprise:

a) Exploring the shoreline with the wind in your hair while jet skiing is an exhilarating experience.

b) Try your hand at stand-up paddling and take in the sea from a different angle as you float over its surface.

c) Parasailing: Take to the sky and fly through the air affixed to a parasail while you take in the breathtaking vistas of Nice from above.

d) Exploring the underwater splendors of the Mediterranean Sea via snorkeling and diving tours. Investigate thriving underwater ecosystems and underwater scenery.

e) Boat Tours: Take a boat trip to see the beautiful coastline, stop at adjacent islands, and take advantage of swimming and tanning in private bays.

5.3 Hiking and Nature Trail

Nice provides a variety of hiking and nature routes for outdoor lovers to enjoy. Among the prominent choices are:

a) From the Old Town to the Promenade des Anglais lies the urban park known as the Promenade du Paillon. It has gorgeous gardens, water features, and lush green areas, creating a tranquil oasis right in the middle of the city.

b) East of Nice is a place called Mont Boron, which has beautiful hiking paths and sweeping ocean views. Walking through this natural park will allow you to discover the Mediterranean flora and animals.

c) Mercantour National Park: Visit the close-by Mercantour National Park for a more thrilling experience. From short strolls to strenuous hikes, this gorgeous park's hiking paths showcase spectacular mountain panoramas, alpine lakes, and a variety of species.

5.4 Cycling Routes

Nice is a bike-friendly city with a variety of routes for cyclists of all skill levels. Several well-liked routes are:

a) Promenade des Anglais: Enjoy the sea air and the stunning vistas of the Mediterranean while riding lazily along the famous Promenade des Anglais.

b) The Voie Verte is a designated bicycle path that follows an ancient railway line. It offers a beautiful journey through rural areas, vineyards, and quaint towns.

c) Col de Vence: Take on the climb to Col de Vence for a strenuous ride. Beautiful views of the surrounding mountains and landscape are available from this well-known climb.

d) Cap d'Antibes: Ride a bicycle through the picturesque coastal roads to explore the lovely Cap d'Antibes peninsula. Take in the vistas of the glistening water and opulent mansions.

5.5 Gardens and Parks

Nice has several parks and gardens for leisure in addition to the beach and nature paths. Among the prominent ones are:

a) Parc Phoenix is a botanical garden and zoological park that is perfect for families since it is home to a range of different plants, flowers, and animals.

b) A tranquil haven in the heart of the city, Jardin Albert Ier is a well-kept park with fountains, statues, and lovely flower beds next to Place Massena.

c) The Jardin de la Colline du Château is a park that gives breathtaking views of Nice and the surrounding area from Castle Hill. It's the ideal location for a walk or a picnic.

d) Parc Chambrun is a park with Mediterranean flora, shaded pathways, and a playground that is situated in the Cimiez district. It offers a tranquil setting for outdoor recreation and relaxation.

Visit Nice's stunning beaches, partake in water sports, explore the city's hiking trails, go cycling along scenic roads, and explore the city's serene parks and gardens to enjoy the great outdoors. Everyone will be able to enjoy the natural beauty of this exciting beachfront location.

Chapter 6: Cultural Experiences

6.1 Galleries and Museums

Nice is a city with a vibrant cultural scene, and it is home to several museums and art galleries that provide insights into its past and creative traditions. Among the prominent ones are:

a) Musée Matisse: Located in the Cimiez district, this museum displays the creations of famous artist Henri Matisse, who spent some time living in Nice. The museum has a sizable collection of sculptures, drawings, and paintings.

b) Musée Marc Chagall: This museum showcases a variety of Marc Chagall's tapestries, stained glass windows, paintings, and paintings with biblical themes.

c) Yves Klein and Niki de Saint Phalle are among the modern and contemporary artists whose works are on display in the Musée d'Art Moderne et d'Art Contemporain (MAMAC).

d) The Musée d'Histoire et d'Art de Nice, which displays the history of the city via a variety of artworks, antiques, and historical documents, is located in the old mansion known as Mansion Masséna.

6.2 Festivals and Other Events

Nice has a variety of festivals and events all year long to recognize its rich cultural diversity and creative prowess. Several notable occasions include:

a) Nice Carnival: One of the biggest carnivals in the world, the Nice Carnival takes place every February. During this thrilling festival, the city is overrun by colorful parades, brilliant floats, and energetic street acts.

b) For the famed Nice Jazz Festival, which takes place in July, music lovers assemble. Jazz performers from all over the world will be performing at this event, which will bring a wide variety of music fans.

c) The Nice International Cinematic Festival honors its cinematic legacy as the birthplace of Auguste Lumière, the father of cinema. It draws both filmmakers and movie lovers since it features a large variety of foreign films.

d) Fête de la Musique: On June 21st each year, artists of many kinds play on the streets, bringing the city to life with music and fostering a celebratory mood.

6.3 Theater and Opera

In Nice, there are several possibilities for culture lovers to take in opera and theatrical events. Consider visiting the following places:

a) The famous opera theatre Opéra Nice Côte d'Azur offers a varied schedule of operas, ballets, classical concerts, and other performing arts events.

b) Théâtre National de Nice: This theater presents both regional and international artists and presents a broad variety of theatrical performances, including modern plays, classics, and experimental works.

6.4 Local Customs and Protocol

To respect the culture and its people, it is important to be informed of Nicene traditions and etiquette while visiting:

a) In formal situations, a handshake is a typical form of greeting. A simple "Bonjour" (Good morning/afternoon) would do in more informal settings.

b) Although Nice's dress code is largely informal, it is appreciated when visitors dress correctly when visiting upmarket restaurants and holy places. Swimwear needs to be restricted to beach regions.

c) Dining: It's traditional to hold off on starting your meal until the host has finished his or her at a restaurant. Additionally, unless it is suitable (such as with finger foods), it is polite to use utensils rather than your hands while eating.

d) Language: While English is widely spoken by residents in tourist regions, using simple French expressions like "Bonjour," "Merci" (thank you), and "S'il vous plaît" (please) is appreciated.

e) Tipping: In restaurants, the bill often includes a service fee. A tiny gratuity is still appreciated for excellent service, however. Taxi drivers, hotel workers, and tour guides all get tips.

You'll develop stronger bonds with the inhabitants and obtain a better understanding of the city's history if you observe traditions and participate in Nice's cultural offerings.

Chapter 7: Shopping in Nice

7.1 Popular Shopping Areas

There are many different retail areas to discover in Nice, which has a diversified shopping environment. Here are a few well-known examples:

a) The lively Avenue Jean Médecin is surrounded by retailers, department stores, and trendy boutiques in the heart of the city. It's an excellent location to discover both local and international fashion.

b) Rue de France is a pedestrian-only street that runs along the Promenade des Anglais and is well-known for its fashion boutiques, jewelry shops, and gift shops. It's a great place to roam about while shopping.

c) Rue Masséna is a lovely street in the center of Nice's Old Town with a mix of traditional businesses, artisanal boutiques, and independent retailers providing apparel, accessories, and regional goods.

7.2 Local Markets

A great experience that lets you fully feel the city's lively culture is exploring the local markets in Nice. Some important marketplaces are listed below:

a) The Old Town's Cours Saleya Market is a vibrant attraction that shouldn't be missed. Fresh foods, flowers, spices, regional delicacies, and handcrafted goods are all available there. Don't miss the flower market's lively atmosphere.

b) Liberation Market: This daily market is well-liked by residents and is located in the Liberation area. Fresh fruits, vegetables, dairy, shellfish, and other locally produced goods are all included. It's a terrific location for neighborhood shopping.

c) Antique Market: The Antique Market, which takes place every Monday in the Cours Saleya, is a haven for collectors of antiques. Explore a great assortment of antique goods, such as jewelry, literature, paintings, and furniture.

7.3 Souvenirs and Unique Finds

Nice provides a variety of possibilities for souvenirs and one-of-a-kind items that encapsulate the spirit of the city and the French Riviera. Here are a few concepts:

a) The city of Nice is renowned for its perfumeries, where you can get a wide selection of distinctive scents made there. Visit perfume counters and choose a smell that makes you think of your stay in Nice.

b) Provencal items: Purchase regional goods like lavender items, olive oil, tapenade, herbes de Provence, or locally made wines to bring a flavor of Provence home.

c) In the Old Town or art galleries, you may find local craftspeople and their masterpieces. Look for items that capture the region's creative essence, such as handcrafted jewelry, pottery, paintings, or one-of-a-kind artwork.

d) Beachwear and Accessories: Given its seaside setting, Nice is a fantastic spot to shop for fashionable swimwear, caps, and accessories. For stylish discoveries, peruse the shops along the Promenade des Anglais.

e) Treat yourself to some regional specialties to enjoy at home or to give as gifts to others. Socca mix, handcrafted chocolates, or Niçoise olive tapenade are a few local delights to think about buying.

To make your shopping experience in Nice more pleasurable and gratifying, keep in mind to browse various stores, assess costs, and interact with regional sellers.

Chapter 8: Practical Travel Information and Tips

8.1 Health and Safety Tips

Your health and safety should come first when you visit Nice. Observe the following advice:

a) Drink lots of water to remain hydrated since the Mediterranean region may become quite hot, particularly in the summer.

b) Sun protection: Cover yourself with sunscreen, a hat, and sunglasses to shield yourself from the sun. During the warmest parts of the day, seek shade.

c) Personal Safety: As in any city, stay aware of your surroundings and watch out for your possessions, particularly in congested places and on public transportation.

d) Know your neighborhood's emergency numbers, including 112 for non-medical emergencies and 15 for medical emergencies.

e) COVID-19 Precautions: Keep up with the most recent COVID-19 recommendations and abide by health and safety precautions such as wearing masks, keeping a social distance, and often washing your hands.

8.2 Communication and Language

French is the official language of Nice. Even if the majority of the population speaks English, learning a few fundamental French words might help you communicate better and better understand the local culture.

8.3 Practical Phrases and Pronunciations

Here are 20 practical French expressions along with their pronunciation:

- ★ Hello - Bonjour (bohn-zhoor)
- ★ Thank you - Merci (mehr-see)
- ★ Please - S'il vous plaît (seel-voo-pleh)
- ★ Excuse me - Excusez-moi (ehks-kew-zay-mwah)
- ★ Yes - Oui (wee)
- ★ No - Non (nohn)
- ★ Sorry - Pardon (par-dohn)
- ★ I don't understand - Je ne comprends pas (zhuh nuh kohn-prahn pah)
- ★ Do you speak English? - Parlez-vous anglais? (par-lay voo ahn-glay)
- ★ Where is...? - Où est...? (ooh ay)

★ How much does it cost? - Combien ça coûte? (kohn-byahn sah koot)

★ I would like... - Je voudrais... (zhuh voo-dreh)

★ Can you help me? - Pouvez-vous m'aider? (poo-vez voo may-day)

★ I'm sorry - Je suis désolé(e) (zhuh swee day-zoh-lay)

★ Goodbye - Au revoir (oh ruh-vwahr)

★ Cheers! - Santé! (sahn-tay)

★ Where is the restroom? - Où sont les toilettes? (ooh sohn lay twah-let)

★ I love Nice - J'adore Nice (zhah-dohr nees)

★ Can I have the bill, please? - L'addition, s'il vous plaît (lah-dee-syon seel-voo-pleh)

★ Have a nice day! - Bonne journée! (buhn zhoor-nay)

8.4 Connectivity and the Internet

Most places in Nice have dependable internet access. Many hotels, eateries, cafés, and public places provide free Wi-Fi. If you need mobile internet, think about getting a local SIM card or ask your service provider about global data packages.

8.5 Family-Friendly Vacation Tips

Here are some suggestions and recommendations for family travelers visiting Nice:

a) Plan family-friendly activities: Nice has a variety of family-friendly attractions, including parks, museums with interactive exhibits, and the Promenade des Anglais. Plan activities based on your research and the interests of the kids.

b) Beach Safety: While visiting the beaches, be aware of any beach safety regulations and keep an eye out for young people. Stay hydrated, use sunscreen, and keep an eye on kids near the water.

c) Nice's main center and several popular tourist destinations are stroller-friendly. Cobblestone streets may be uneven in certain older portions of the city. For better navigation, think about utilizing a small, mobile stroller.

d) Kid-Friendly Dining: Seek eateries with kids' menus or with a good standing among families.

Many restaurants provide high chairs or booster seats as a courtesy to young guests.

e) Local parks and playgrounds: Make use of the parks and play areas offered by the city. They provide kids the chance to play and expend energy while enjoying the great outdoors.

8.6 Nice for Solo Travelers

Here are some suggestions for Nice single visitors to make their trip fun and secure:

a) Safety Advice: If you're traveling alone, be wary of your surroundings, particularly at night. Keep to well-lit locations, conceal expensive stuff, and let someone know your destination.

b) Join scheduled excursions, stay in hostels, or take part in social activities to connect with other visitors. It might improve your experience and provide chances for group activities.

c) Investigate the communities: Get to know Nice's many communities to choose locations that suit your interests and preferences. Pick hotels in locations with good transportation options.

d) Trust Your Instincts: When talking with people or selecting which regions to investigate, trust your instincts and utilize common sense. Remove yourself from a situation if it makes you feel unsafe or uneasy.

e) Interact with the community to learn about their culture. Respect others, have an open mind, and seize the chance to interact with the neighborhood.

8.7 Romantic Adventure Tip

Here are some suggestions for couples looking for romantic encounters in Nice:

a) Romantic strolls are recommended at sunset along the Promenade des Anglais or the seaside. A romantic atmosphere is created by the breathtaking sights and soft sea wind.

b) Romantic Dinners: Spend a special evening with your partner with a candlelight meal at one of Nice's exquisite restaurants or by the sea.

c) Boat Tours: Set off on a charming boat excursion around the French Riviera to explore quaint bays and take in the scenery. For a spectacular experience, think about going on a sunset cruise.

d) Wine sampling: For a wine-tasting experience, go to a nearby vineyard in Nice's countryside. Enjoy the aromas of local wines and the enchanting ambiance.

e) Spa Day for Couples: Indulge in a romantic spa day for two at one of the city's opulent wellness facilities. Together, unwind and indulge in relaxing spa services.

f) Plan a day trip or weekend break to one of the neighboring romantic locales, such as the quaint town of Eze or the opulent city of Cannes. These lovely settings provide a romantic setting for important occasions.

Nice provides a variety of romantic experiences for couples to appreciate, whether you're touring the city, having private meals, or taking in the splendor of the French Riviera.

Chapter 9: Suggested Itineraries

9.1 One day in Nice

Here is a recommended plan to help you make the most of your time if you only have one day to see Nice:

Morning:

- Take a walk along the Promenade des Anglais in the morning and take in the stunning views of the Mediterranean Sea.

- Explore the Old Town (Vieux Nice) with its winding lanes, quaint shops, and vibrant structures.

- Visit the Cours Saleya Market to take in the lively ambiance and try some local cuisine.

Afternoon:

- For sweeping views of Nice, go to Castle Hill (Colline du Château). Either use a trek or an elevator to ascend.

- Visit the Musee Matisse to see the famous artist Henri Matisse's creations.

- Enjoy a leisurely lunch at one of the neighborhood cafés while sampling some traditional Nice fare.

Evening:

- Place Massena is a bustling area with lovely fountains and a lively atmosphere. Spend the evening there.

- Visit a neighboring shopping area to indulge in some retail therapy or unwind at a sidewalk café.

- Spend a special evening together at one of Nice's best restaurants to cap off the day.

9.2 A Three-Day Visit to Nice

You may tour the neighboring regions and get deeper into the city's highlights with three days in Nice. Here is a recommended route:

Day 1:

Observe the "One Day in Nice" plan as outlined above.

Day 2:

- Spend the day at Monaco, which is close by the rail from Nice. Visit the renowned Casino de Monte-Carlo, explore the opulent city-state, and take in the breathtaking views from the Prince's Palace.

- Return to Nice in the evening to take part in one of the city's exciting pubs or nightclubs.

Day 3:

- Spend the day exploring Nice's local attractions and hidden gems:

- Discover the Cours Saleya Market and indulge in some regional specialties.

- Get some peace and tranquility and enjoy the sights by going to the Parc de la Colline du Château.

- Visit the bustling Nice Port neighborhood and take it easy for lunch at one of the waterfront eateries.

- To admire modern and contemporary art, go to the MAMAC Museum of Modern and Contemporary Art.

9.3 A Seven Day in Nice

You may spend more time in Nice, the surrounding cities, and the French Riviera if you stay for a week. Here is a recommended route:

Day 1-3:
Observe the "Three Days in Nice" agenda that was previously described.

Day 4:
- Take a day trip to Cannes, which is renowned for its glitzy vibe and

gorgeous beaches. Visit the Palais des Festivals, wander along the La Croisette promenade, and explore the city.

Day 5:

- Visit the lovely town of Antibes, which is situated between Nice and Cannes. Visit the Picasso Museum, stroll around the historic district, and relax on a sandy beach.

Day 6:

- Visit the charming hamlet of Eze for a day. Discover the quaint shops and galleries while strolling through the ancient alleyways and the renowned Jardin Exotique with its stunning vistas.

Day 7:

- Visit the beautiful beach town of Saint-Tropez for the day. Enjoy the splendor, go to the stunning beaches, and discover the lively waterfront.

This program offers a variety of cultural discoveries, scenic splendor, and enjoyable encounters throughout the French Riviera, allowing you to enjoy the finest of Nice and its surroundings.

Chapter 10: Conclusion

10.1 Final Thoughts

It's time to think back on the experiences and recollections you've had as you come to the end of your trip to Nice. Nice is a city that provides the ideal fusion of natural beauty, history, culture, and a lively environment. Every tourist will find something to enchant them in Nice, from the breathtaking Promenade des Anglais to the quaint alleyways of the Old Town.

You've had the opportunity to check out famous sites including Castle Hill, the Musee Matisse, and Place Massena during your vacation. You've savored the regional food, taken part in the energetic nightlife, and found undiscovered attractions that capture the city's genuine character.

Nice will always remain etched in your vacation memories, whether it was walking along the beaches, participating in water sports, or taking in the local culture and artistic attractions.

Take note of the facts you learned from this travel guide, whether it pertains to the ideal time to go, visa requirements, or beneficial knowledge like language hints and helpful phrases. Make the most of your visit by interacting with the people and navigating the city with ease with this information.

11.2 Safe travels!

We wish you a wonderful and safe journey as you say goodbye to Nice. May your experiences in Nice serve as a lasting inspiration for your future journeys. Keep in mind the learning experiences, culinary delights, and French Riviera beauty.

Keep the spirit of adventure with you whether you're going farther on your trip or going back home. Let your experiences in Nice serve as a reminder that many marvels in the world are just waiting to be discovered. Good luck and may your travels bring you pleasure, exploration, and wonderful experiences!

Bon Voyage!!!!

Printed in Great Britain
by Amazon

26066200R00046